Mel Bay Presents

Easy Classics for TRUMPET

With Piano Accompaniment

Piano Accompaniments
by **Jannette Spitzer**
and **Laura Spitzer**

Selected and Arranged
by **Peter Spitzer**

The *Easy Classics* books were written to provide beginning to intermediate instrumentalists with an enjoyable introduction to some of the great classic melodies.

The flute, clarinet, alto sax, tenor sax, and trumpet parts are fully compatible, and may be played in any combination, with or without piano accompaniment. (Note to the pianist: Solo and duet parts are shown in the upper staff, in concert key. For some instruments, actual pitch may be in a lower octave.)

The violin book is transposed to keys suitable for that instrument, and has its own accompaniment.

Peter Spitzer

Contents

		Solo/Duet	Piano
Ode to Joy	Beethoven	4	2
Sleeping Beauty Waltz	Tchaikovsky	6	4
Eine Kleine Nachtmusik	Mozart	8	7
Adagio (from Clarinet Concerto)	Mozart	10	10
Hungarian Dance #5	Brahms	12	12
Emperor Hymn	Haydn	14	14
The Trout	Schubert	16	16
Theme from Polovetsian Dances	Borodin	17	18
Scheherazade	Rimsky-Korsakov	18	20
Jesu, Joy of Man's Desiring	Bach	19	22
Radetzky March	Strauss	20	23
Cancan	Offenbach	22	26
Habanera	Bizet	24	29
Toreador Song	Bizet	26	32
O Sole Mio	di Capua	28	34
William Tell Overture	Rossini	30	36

1 2 3 4 5 6 7 8 9 0

Ode to Joy
from Symphony #9

Moderato

Ludwig van Beethoven (1770-1827)

2

Sleeping Beauty Waltz

from the ballet "Sleeping Beauty"

Peter Ilich Tchaikovsky (1843-1890)

Eine Kleine Nachtmusik
from Serenade K. 525

Wolfgang Amadeus Mozart (1756-1791)

Allegro moderato

7

Adagio
from Clarinet Concerto, K. 622

Wolfgang Amadeus Mozart (1756-1791)

Hungarian Dance #5

Johannes Brahms (1833-1897)

Emperor Hymn

Franz Joseph Haydn (1732-1809)

Maestoso

The Trout

Franz Schubert (1797-1828)

Moderato

Theme from Polovetsian Dances
from the opera "Prince Igor"

Alexander Borodin (1833-1887)

Scheherazade

Andante

Nicholas Rimsky-Korsakov (1844-1908)

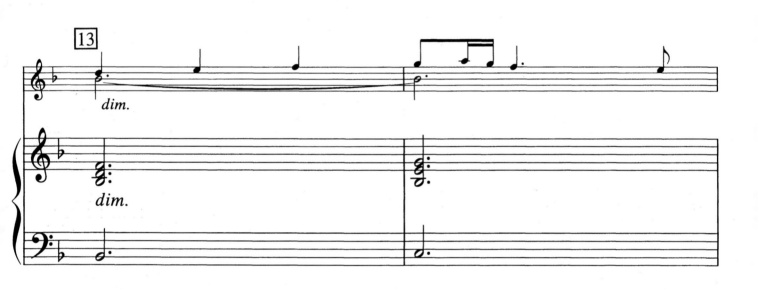

Jesu, Joy of Man's Desiring
from Cantata No. 147

Johann Sebastian Bach (1685-1750)

Radetzky March

Johann Strauss (1804-1849)

Cancan
from the opera "Orpheus in the Underworld"

Jacques Offenbach (1819-1880)

27

Habanera
from the opera "Carmen"

Georges Bizet (1838-1875)

30

Toreador Song
from the opera "Carmen"

Georges Bizet (1838-1875)

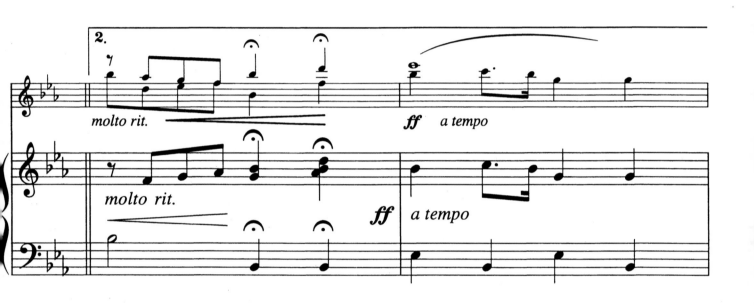

O Sole Mio

Slowly, with feeling

Eduardo di Capua (1864-1917)

William Tell Overture
from the opera "William Tell"

Gioacchino Rossini (1792-1868)

Great Music at Your Fingertips